T0015502

It is said that the original name of Butterfly Spring was Bottomless Pond. A man named Old Zhang, a woodcutter, lived beside the pond with his daughter Wengu. The father and daughter depended on each other, and lived a hard but happy life.

One day, Old Zhang and Wengu went to the mountains to cut firewood. Suddenly, Wengu saw a young, wounded deer running towards her. The deer fell to the ground, crying.

Wengu bent down to see what was wrong with the deer and found an arrow in its body. After a while, a young hunter came running, with a bow and an arrow in his hands.

Wengu held the deer tightly in her arms and begged the hunter to let her take care of it. The hunter, called Xialang, accepted the request, and even took out medicine from his medicine bag and applied it on the wound. Xialang and Wengu fell in love at first sight.

After that, the two young people always met by the pond, would sing together, and fell in love. As a token of her love to Xialang, Wengu gave him a "100-butterfly embroidery" that she made herself.

At that time, Dali Town was ruled by King Yu, who had long admired Wengu's beauty. One day, he asked for Old Zhang's permission to marry her, but Wengu refused.

King Yu could not stand being rejected by Wengu. Then one of the king's assistants came up with an idea: they ordered Wengu to the palace to make an embroidery with 100 butterflies. When they brought her to the palace, she would remain a prisoner there.

Soon the king's soldiers besieged Old Zhang's home. Wengu understood the king's evil plan and refused to leave her home. Old Zhang and Wengu had no choice but to fight the soldiers.

The little deer saw this and immediately ran into the mountains to look for Xialang. It took his sash in its mouth and dragged him down the mountain.

When Xialang got to Old Zhang's house, he found Old Zhang badly injured, lying on the ground and dying. But before he died, Old Zhang told Xialang everything. Upon hearing what had happened, Xialang was very angry! He buried Old Zhang, took his bow and arrows and his sword, and galloped on his horse to King Yu's palace to save his sweetheart.

When Xialang arrived at the palace, he saw that the high walls were tightly guarded, so he hid by the wall and waited for the right opportunity. That night, although the lanterns on the high towers were lit up, Xialang was able to sneak into the palace under the cover of darkness.

There were countless pavilions and winding hallways in King Yu's palace. Xialang had never been to the palace. How could he find Wengu? Soon, he had lost his way. He took out his "100-butterfly embroidery" and just at that moment, he could hear a faint song from afar. It sounded just like Wengu's voice!

Xialang's spirits soared, and following the song, he continued to look for Wengu. Because he had to stay away from the patrol guards in the king's palace, he moved slowly all the way. With every step, Xialang became more and more anxious.

Finally the song led Xialang to a separate pavilion. Xialang looked up, the pavilion lights were bright. He could hear a commanding voice ceaselessly questioning Wengu. But Wengu did not answer. She just kept singing the familiar song. How Xialang wished to break into the house to save Wengu! But instinctively, he knew that there were too many guards in the room. He had to calm down and wait for the right moment. For every minute he had to wait, it felt like a sharp knife stabbing his heart.

In an angry rage, King Yu finally left with his guards. Xialang pushed open the door and quickly rushed into the room. Wengu was hanging from a rope!

Xialang cut down the rope,
lifted Wengu onto his back,
and rushed out of the palace.

The patrol guards discovered Xialang and Wengu as they were escaping. They started chasing them and did all they could to kill them. Xialang fought all the way and soon, wounds, large and small, were

Eventually, Xialang and Wengu arrived at Bottomless Pond. Xialang had no arrows left and his sword was broken. They had no way out, surrounded by King Yu's guards.

Finding nowhere else to run, Xialang and Wengu looked at each other, and smiled.
Singing their song, they jumped into Bottomless Pond. Suddenly, a pair of colorful
butterflies flew out of the pond. Following the pair of butterflies were countless
colorful smaller butterflies. People believed that the big pair of colorful butterflies
were the incarnations of Xialang and Wengu, and the small butterflies were from
their love token, the "100-butterfly embroidery." The scene was colorful and
spectacular, and Bottomless Pond was renamed Butterfly Spring.

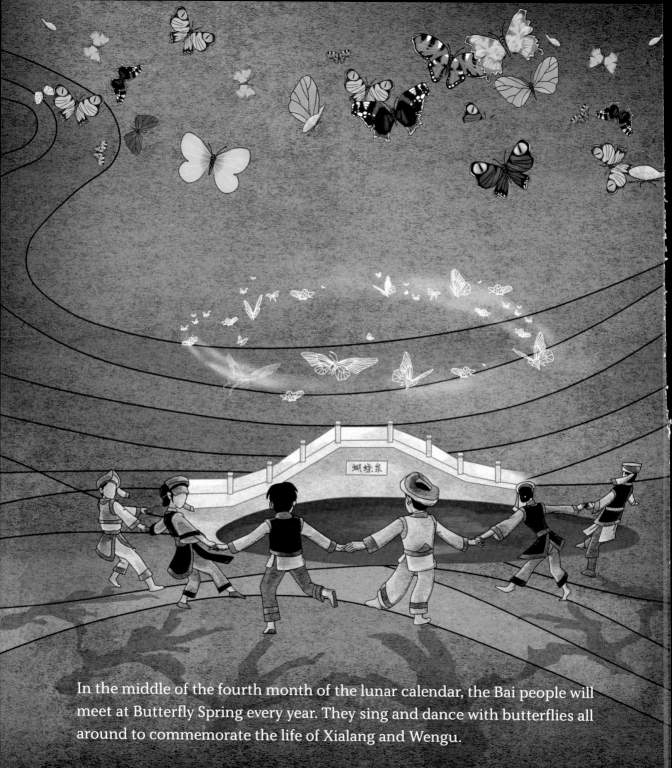

In the middle of the fourth month of the lunar calendar, the Bai people will meet at Butterfly Spring every year. They sing and dance with butterflies all around to commemorate the life of Xialang and Wengu.